Dian Fossey

and the
Mountain Gorillas

by Jane A. Schott
illustrations by Ralph L. Ramstad

Carolrhoda Books, Inc./Minneapolis

*For Maxine Allen, loving aunt, dear friend, and my
strong support* — *J.A.S.*

*For the friends and defenders of wildlife the world
over* — *R.L.R.*

The photograph on page 47 appears with the permission of Corbis-Bettman.

Text copyright © 2000 by Carolrhoda Books, Inc.
Illustrations copyright © 2000 by Ralph L. Ramstad

Carolrhoda Books, Inc.
A Division of Lerner Publishing Group
241 First Avenue North
Minneapolis, MN 55401 U.S.A.

Website address: www.lernerbooks.com

Library of Congress Cataloging-in-Publication Data

Schott, Jane A., 1946–
    Dian Fossey and the mountain gorillas / by Jane A. Schott ; illustrated by
Ralph L. Ramstad.
       p. cm. — (On my own biography)
    Summary: Biography of the American woman who spent eighteen years
in Rwanda, Africa, studying mountain gorillas and working for their
survival.
    ISBN 1-57505-082-X (lib. bdg. : alk. paper)
    1. Fossey, Dian—Juvenile literature. 2. Primatologists—United
States—Biography—Juvenile literature. [1. Fossey, Dian.
2. Zoologists. 3. Gorilla. 4. Women—Biography] I. Ramstad,
Ralph L., 1919– ill. II. Title. III. Series.
QL31.F65S36 2000
599.884'092—dc21
    [B]   99-33161

Manufactured in the United States of America
1 2 3 4 5 6 – JR – 05 04 03 02 01 00

Louisville, Kentucky
1960

"It's not fair," thought Dian.
"Mary is going on a safari to Africa,
and I want to go, too!"
Dian Fossey was standing on the front step
of her little house in Kentucky.

Birds were singing.

The sun was shining brightly.

But 28-year-old Dian

was not feeling sunny.

She had just talked to her friend Mary.

And Mary's news

had not made Dian happy.

Dian jumped off the step.

Out across the green fields she ran,

faster and faster

until she was out of breath.

Then she fell down in the long grass.

Three of her dogs raced up behind her.

They licked her face and hands

until she sat up and laughed.

Dian remembered how lonely she had been
when she was a little girl.
Her mother and stepfather had not let her
have pets.
"At least I have pets now," she thought.
Dian looked into the friendly eyes
of the dogs around her.
She really loved animals.
Maybe more than people.

It was too bad that Mary would be going
to Africa without her.
Dian had often dreamed of seeing
all the wild animals there.
But it cost a lot of money to go to Africa.
Dian decided to save money so she could go
in a few years.

Dian began to read books about Africa.

One book told about mountain gorillas.

Only about 300 mountain gorillas were left.

They lived in one small spot in Africa.

Many had been hurt by hunters' traps.

Sometimes they were so badly hurt,

they died.

Sometimes hunters killed the gorillas

with their spears.

Would mountain gorillas soon

be gone forever?

Dian hoped not.

She wanted to learn more about them.

She decided to see the mountain gorillas

when she went to Africa.

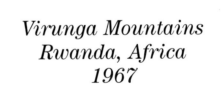

Virunga Mountains
Rwanda, Africa
1967

As soon as Dian saw the meadow,

her heart began to sing.

Climbing up mountains in Africa

was very hard.

Dian felt as though her lungs would burst.

Her legs and feet were tired and sore.
But at last she had found a wonderful place
to make her camp.
Dian put down the heavy pack.
She found a little stream and splashed
cold water on her hands and face.

All around the camp
she could see mountains.
She turned one way
and saw Mount Karisimbi.
She turned another way
and saw Mount Visoke.

She put the names of the two mountains
together—Karisoke.
That is what she would call this place.

The men who helped carry her packs
set up the camp.

They put up tents to sleep in.

They found wood to build a fire.

Soon they were opening cans of food.

The smell of cooking filled the camp.

Dian sat down on a fallen log.
She was tired and hungry,
but she was happy.
Karisoke would be her new home.
She was there to study
the mountain gorillas.

Dian stared at the trees
beyond the meadow.
Their leaves made a thick curtain.
She could not see the mountain gorillas
that lived there.
But she could hardly wait to look for them.
She would begin the next day.

She would write down everything
she saw gorillas doing.
She would take pictures of them.
She would make tape recordings
of the sounds they made.
Since only about 300 were left,
Dian wanted to help keep them safe.

Gorillas

Dian walked along the forest trail.

She had come this way to see the gorillas

many times before.

Carefully she stepped

through the wet leaves.

Her big boots were hard to keep quiet.

But they helped her feet stay warm and dry.

Dian wore a plastic poncho

to keep the rain off her clothes.

Still, she was cold and damp.

Her binoculars hung around her neck.

In her pocket were her notebook and pen.

Dian heard a crashing sound.

She stopped walking

and became very quiet.

Then the noise stopped.

All she could hear was rain dripping

from the trees.

Dian waited.

She knew gorillas had made the noise.

They were moving through the trees

looking for plants to eat.

Dian must not get too close

and scare them.

Suddenly, the crashing noise came again.

Dian used a big knife she carried.

She cut a walking space

between the thick plants.

She must keep up with the gorillas.

Once they finished eating,

they would move on.

Carefully she took a few steps.

There they were.

A family was gathered under a large tree.

They were eating leaves.

Their hair was long and black and shiny
with rain.

Some of the gorillas reached up
to grab leaves.

Others walked around the tree on their feet
and the knuckles of their hands.

Their faces were all different.

To remember each face,

Dian had given the gorillas names.

A big male gorilla sat under the tree.

He was much larger than Dian.

Beethoven was his name.

Effie and Marchessa sat close to him

with their babies.

Playing nearby were Icarus and Piper.

As Dian sat down to watch, a stick cracked.

Beethoven jumped up.

He looked at Dian.

The hair on his huge head stood up.

Then he began to pound his chest.

Poka, poka, pok!

"Hoot, hoot, hoot!" he cried.

The other gorillas jumped up, too.

But Dian was not afraid.

She knew that Beethoven

was only trying to scare her away.

Slowly, Dian picked a leaf
and pretended to eat it.
Beethoven watched her.
After a few minutes, he began to eat again.
Soon all the gorillas were eating.

Dian had learned that these animals
were usually shy and quiet.
Gorillas did not attack people
unless they were threatened.
They lived in family groups.
They ate leaves, not animals or people.
Dian took her notebook and pen
from her pocket.
She began to write down
everything she saw the gorillas do.

That night, Dian was up very late.

Inside her little shack, the lantern made

a bright spot in the dark night.

Dian had no electric lights, bathroom,

or television.

She did not want these things.

Her wet clothes hung over

a little oil heater.

Her dog, Cindy, lay by her feet.

Her pet monkey, Kima,

sat on the table beside her typewriter.

Tap, tap, tap, tap, tap.

Dian typed out everything she had written

in the forest.

This work was the hardest

she had ever done in her whole life.

Her hands and face were scratched.

Her leg muscles ached.

Her ankle throbbed from where

she had caught it in a big vine.

But these things did not matter to Dian.

She was happy at Karisoke.

Digit

One day, Dian stood behind a tree.
With her binoculars,
she was watching a gorilla family.
One young gorilla was playing
among the leaves.

The young gorilla's middle finger
was twisted.

Perhaps it had once been broken.

Dian named him Digit.

Then a big male gorilla saw Dian.

"Hoot, hoot!" he called.

All the gorillas quickly ran away.

After that, Dian began to look for Digit
when she went into the forest.
She often saw him playing alone.
There were no other gorillas Digit's age
in his family.
Soon Digit began to watch for Dian.
He seemed to enjoy her visits.

One day Dian took a mirror with her.

She set the mirror down in the forest

where Digit would find it.

Then she stepped back to watch.

Digit saw the mirror.

He lay down and looked at himself.

He squeezed his lips together.

He moved his head from side to side.

"What is he thinking?" Dian wondered.

As Digit grew older,

he was no longer as interested in Dian.

Digit became a leader of his family.

But he was still very special to Dian.

Trouble

Rwanda was a small country
with many people and little food.
When people were hungry,
hunters killed animals in the forests.
They were not allowed to hunt
in the gorillas' forest.
But sometimes they came anyway.

One day, men who worked for Dian
told her that hunters were near.
Dian was afraid the gorillas would be hurt.
She began to search for Digit
and his family.

The next day, she and her men found Digit.

He had tried to save his family

from the hunters.

Digit had been killed.

Dian cried for a long time.

She had known Digit for 10 years.

He was her friend.

The men helped Dian bury Digit

at Karisoke.

Dian was sad, but she was also angry.

The gorillas' forest was supposed

to be guarded.

No hunters were to come in.

But there were not enough guards

to keep the hunters out.

"I must do something myself,"

thought Dian.

She would ask people to give money

to help the gorillas.

She would use the money to pay

for more guards.

Dian named her plan the Digit Fund.

Pictures of Digit were shown on television.
A newscaster told Digit's story.
Some people sent money
to help the gorillas.
But there was not enough to hire
very many guards.
And more hunters were coming
to the forest every day.

Dian knew she had to do more.
She wrote about the gorillas
for newspapers and magazines.
Then she wrote a book
called *Gorillas in the Mist*.
Dian wanted everyone to know
about the gorillas.
Once they knew, people would want
to help save the gorillas.
Dian was sure of it.

Dian traveled all around the world.

She told people about the hunters.

If the killing did not stop soon,

there would be no more mountain gorillas.

Dian was determined that there would

always be mountain gorillas in Rwanda.

People listened to Dian.

They wanted to help.

When Dian went back to Karisoke,
college students came to help her.
They studied the gorillas, too.
Dian trained men from Rwanda
to keep hunters out of the park.
They found and broke the hunters' traps.

People all around the world
were reading Dian's book.
In Rwanda, the people were becoming
proud of their gorillas.
For 18 years, Dian Fossey had worked
to save the mountain gorillas.
She believed they would finally
have a chance to survive.

Afterword

Dian Fossey continued her work with mountain gorillas until 1985. Then, late in December, she was killed. She was 53 years old. Some people think she was killed by one of the hunters who came to the gorillas' forest. But her murderer was never found. Three days later, Dian was buried at Karisoke near the grave of her friend Digit.

During her 18 years at Karisoke, Dian learned more about mountain gorillas than anyone had learned before. And she shared what she learned. Her book, *Gorillas in the Mist*, was read by thousands of people.

Scientists still study the gorillas at Karisoke. Guards keep the hunters out of the gorillas' forest. People from many countries visit the forest to watch the gorillas, but only from a distance. And people around the world know that without Dian Fossey, the mountain gorillas would have been gone forever.

47

Important Dates

January 16, 1932—Dian is born in San Francisco, California.

1935—Dian's parents are divorced.

1937—Dian's mother remarries.

1954—Dian graduates from college and takes a job in Kentucky.

1963—Dian visits Africa for the first time and meets Dr. Louis Leakey, a scientist who studied the earliest humans.

1966—Dian returns to Africa to begin studying the mountain gorillas.

1967—Dian founds the Karisoke research station in Rwanda.

1974—Dian receives a doctorate from Cambridge University.

1983—Dian's book, *Gorillas in the Mist*, is published.

1985—Dian is killed at Karisoke.

2.5

Dian Fossey and the Mountain Gorillas

Schott, Jane A.

Lex: R.L: 2.5   Pts: 2